Pizza Man

Pizza Man

by Marjorie Pillar

Thomas Y. Crowell   New York

Library of Congress Cataloging-in-Publication Data
Pillar, Marjorie.
  Pizza man / by Marjorie Pillar.
     p.   cm.
  Summary: Black and white photographs highlight the steps
in making a pizza pie, from the moment the pizza man starts
mixing the dough until he serves a slice to a hungry customer.
  ISBN 0-690-04836-X : $. — ISBN 0-690-04838-6 : $
  1. Pizza—Juvenile literature.   [1. Pizza.]   I. Title.
TX770.P58P55   1990   89-35526
641.8'24—dc20   CIP
                                                      AC

IN APPRECIATION

for my teacher and mentor, Arthur Leipzig,
who pointed out the road,
and for my family,
whose encouragement helped me to explore it

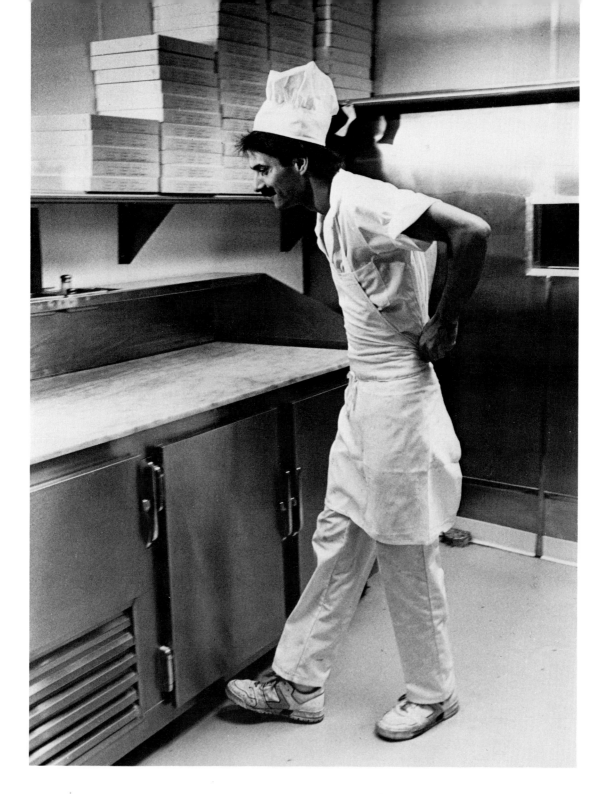

I'm a pizza man.
Let me show you how I make my pies.

I start my day by making the pizza dough.
I use flour,

water,

and yeast.

A large machine does all the mixing.

It churns the ingredients

to make a sticky,
pasty dough.

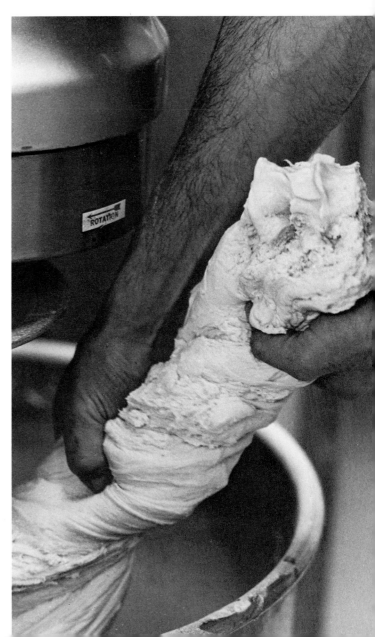

I need help to get the dough
out of the big mixing pot.

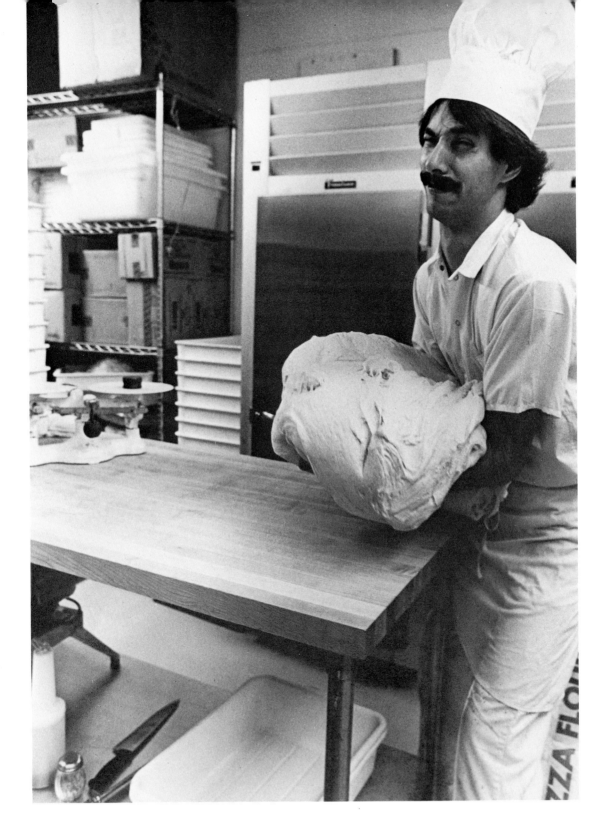

It is really heavy.

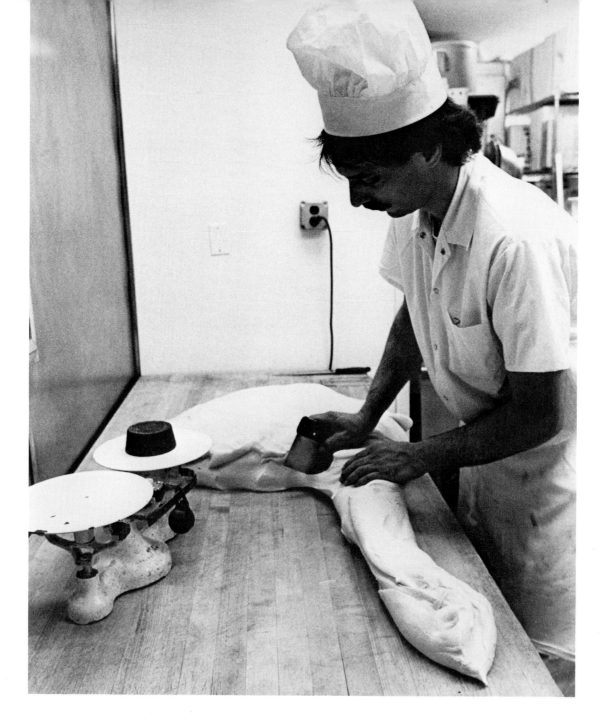

Next I cut and weigh the dough to get the right amount. I check the scale to see if it says 1½ pounds. That's what I need to make a pie.

I don't always cut off
exactly enough dough.

Sometimes
I have to add more,

and more,
until I get it right.

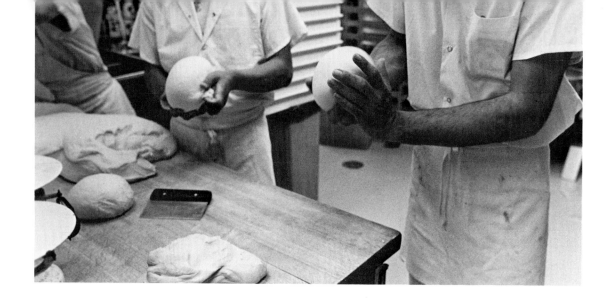

My helper and I make round mounds of dough every morning.

The yeast works to make the dough rise.

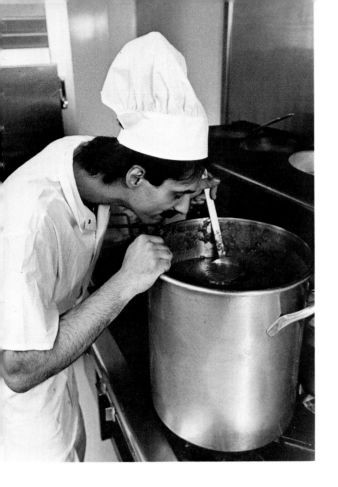

Then I make the
tomato sauce.
My sauce smells
so good.

It tastes
so delicious.

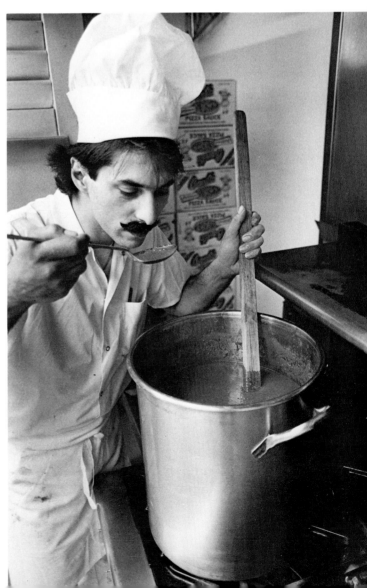

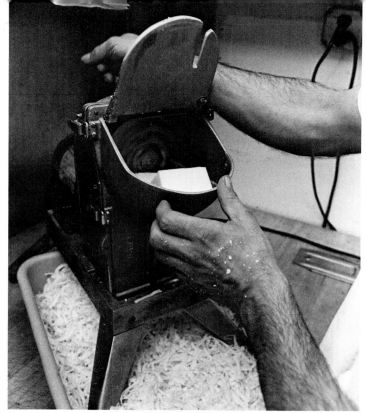

You can't make
a pizza without
cheese!

I cut small chunks
of mozzarella
and shred them
in a special machine.

The fun starts when
someone stops by for a slice,

or phones in an order.
Now it's time to start making pies!

I take a mound
of dough. I begin to
push and pull it into
a flat, round circle.

I toss it into the air
to stretch it even more.

I flip it higher and higher.

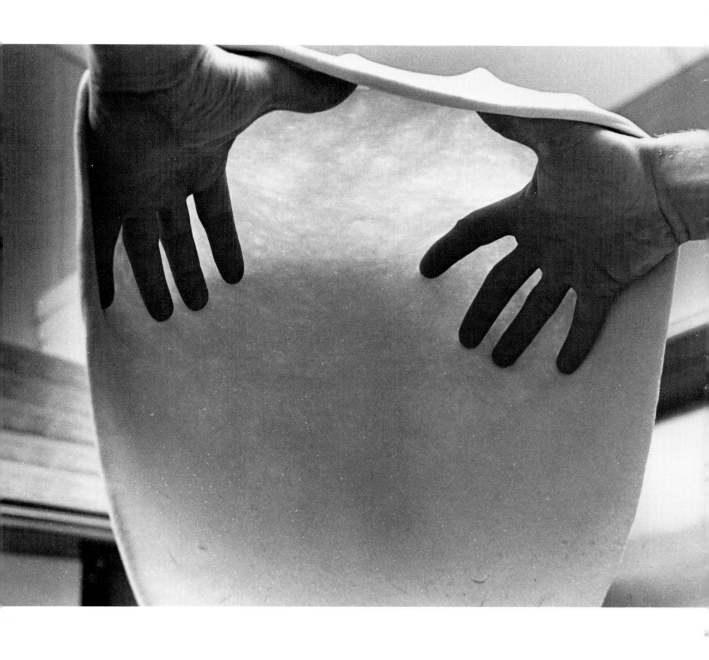

It's almost right.

Oops! Sometimes the dough tears.

No problem.

I can fix it.

When the dough is thin and round enough, it's time to add the sauce.

I spread tomato sauce all over the dough, except for the edges.

This is fun!

I pile the cheese over the sauce.

Some people like to choose their own toppings. They can pick pepperoni, salami, meatballs, olives or maybe mushrooms, peppers, onions or broccoli. Sometimes they combine several toppings. There's room on my pizzas for all of them!

Finally, I bake the pizza in a very hot oven.
I check it while it is baking.

Sometimes I turn it around
to make sure it doesn't burn.

Fifteen minutes and the pizza's done!

I use a pizza cutter to slice the pie.

I love to watch my customers eat my pizza!

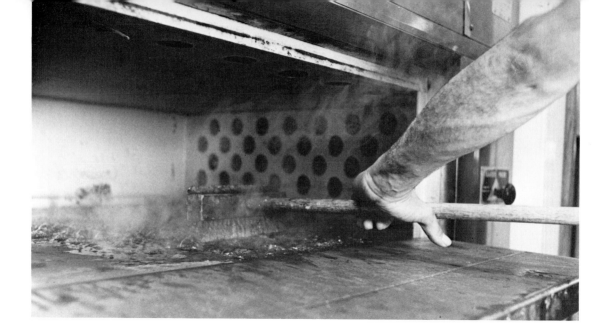

On a busy day, I might make over 100 pizzas. And there's still work to do before I go home. I clean my ovens inside and out.

I have to put together boxes for tomorrow, too. Not everyone eats their pizza in my store. Some customers take it home.

I love baking pizza. I'm a pizza man!